Walking West Dorset

By Robert Hesketh

Inspiring Places Publishing
2 Down Lodge Close
Alderholt
Fordingbridge
Hants
SP6 3JA
www.inspiringplaces.co.uk

ISBN 978-0-9564104-8-1
Contains Ordnance Survey data © Crown copyright and database right (2011)

JURASSICCOAST
QUALITY
BUSINESS

GW00320175

Contents

Page

Note:
A grid reference is given for the start of each walk together with the closest postcode that could be found. Please take the grid reference as the more accurate.

All routes in this book were checked before publication. However, changes (especially to signage) can happen in the countryside over which neither publisher nor author have any control. Please let us know if you experience any major difficulties.

The Coast Path

Parts of the West Dorset Coast Path are unstable and prone to slippages. When these occur, please follow signed diversions. Contact the South West Coast Path Association www.southwestcoastpath.com 01752 896237 or Dorset County Council Rights of Way Team 01305 224463 for up to date information.

Front cover photograph: The path towards Plush. Rear cover photograph: Eggardon Hill. Pages 2 and 3: A view over Beaminster.

Introduction

These circular walks have been selected to help you discover West Dorset's wonderfully varied coast and countryside. They differ in length, but more importantly in terrain, so the time needed to complete will vary from one person to another. But why hurry? Each walk has its own character and there are many viewpoints and places of historical and geological interest en route. Please take them at your own pace and I'm sure you'll enjoy them as much as I have.

Clothing and Footwear

Exploring West Dorset on foot is a pleasure throughout the seasons – so long as you're prepared. Mud, puddles and some rough footing are par for the course, thus walking boots are ideal, but Wellingtons can't breathe or offer ankle support and sandals are inadequate.

The climate's (usually!) mild, but changeable. It's always wise to pack waterproofs and an extra warm layer in your rucksack. Gorse and nettles make trousers a better option than shorts, especially as they provide some protection from ticks, which may carry Lyme disease. If a tick does latch onto you, remove it carefully and promptly with tweezers.

Kit

Even in winter drinking water is essential – allow a litre on short walks, two on longer ones. Walking poles or a stick are a great bonus, ditto extra food and a mobile phone. Use the book's sketch maps as a general guide, but Ordnance Survey Explorer maps for detail. Explorers 116, 117, 129 and OL15 cover the whole area.

The Countryside

Nothing beats walking for safe and healthy exercise, but please remember most cliff paths are unfenced and mind out for uneven and waterlogged ground, especially on the coast path. Please follow the Country Code; respect farmers' crops and leave gates closed or open as you find them and keep dogs under control, particularly during the lambing and bird nesting seasons.

1. Lyme Regis Distance: 8km/5miles, Time: 2 ½ hours, Exertion: Moderate

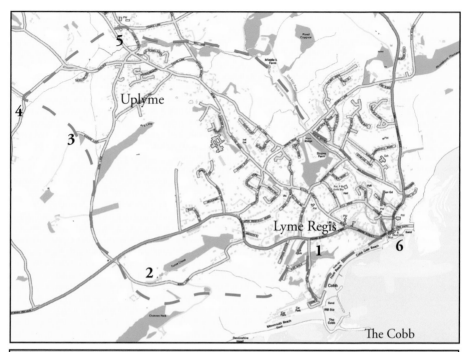

The Cobb

Information
Start: Holmbush car park, Lyme Regis DT7 3HX, SY33668 92032
Terrain: Footpaths, quiet lanes and back streets. Two short, steep ascents, one steep descent.
Stiles: 8
Refreshments: Pub in Uplyme; wide choice of pubs, cafés and restaurants in Lyme Regis.
Public toilets: At start and in Lyme.
Maps: Explorer 116 or Landranger 193

Packed with interest and variety, this circuit of Lyme Regis includes superb views of Dorset's Jurassic Coast and a visit to the Undercliffs, part of the area's remarkable geology that made it Britain's first natural World Heritage Site. Lyme Regis has a particularly rich fossil heritage, which can be explored in its excellent museums. Also en route is Lyme Fossil Shop; the Cobb - Lyme's medieval breakwater – and a restored watermill. Take time to enjoy these, the resort's timeless air and its many extant Georgian buildings, which would be instantly recognizable to the characters of Jane Austen's *Persuasion* and John Fowles' *The French Lieutenant's Woman*.

1. Walk to the lower end of Holmbush car park and join the signed Coast Path. Continue ahead signed "Ware ½" when you reach a path junction. Only 100m ahead, bear left "To Coast Path". Keep ahead "Coast Path Seaton" at the next signpost. Good views onto the Jurassic Coast and the Cobb open out. Spring flowers, including ragged robin, bluebells, bird's foot trefoil and orchids thrive here. Continue on the Coast Path into the Axmouth-Lyme Regis Undercliffs. Turn right "Permissive Path to Chimney Rock". The path winds gently through trees, then climbs steeply up steps to Chimney Rock, a remnant stack of Chert Beds rock.

> **Axmouth-Lyme Regis Undercliffs**
> This 304ha National Nature Reserve was created by a series of dramatic landslips for which the West Dorset and East Devon coast is notorious. Much of the reserve is dense woodland, established by natural succession. One of Britain's finest "wildernesses", they are eerily quiet apart from birdsong and the murmur of insects, though there are areas of open grassland, wetland and scrub too, providing a diversity of habitats.

Continue up more steps. Follow the field path ahead to a stile. Continue to a lane and bear left.

2. Follow the lane to the main road. Cross with care into Gore Lane. After 400m, bear left onto a signed "Public Footpath". Follow the path to a stile. Turn right along the edge of the field. Follow the path steeply downhill to a lane by a house.

3. Turn left. Only 50m ahead, turn right at a junction of paths to cross a stile. Take the signed public footpath almost immediately left. This heads north-west, leading over another stile and the bed of a dismantled railway. Continue downhill to meet a lane at a metal five barred gate. On your left, at a distance of some 500m, are the tall arches of the dismantled railway, the 1903 Axminster to Lyme Regis branch line.

4. Turn right and follow the lane ahead for 450m ignoring side turnings. Fork left. Cross a lane into a drive. Turn right 30m ahead into a public footpath. Continue with the hedge on your left. Follow the edge of the cricket field to the main road. Cross carefully and climb the steps

ahead to the church, where the ancient churchyard yew is said to be 1,000 years old.

5. Turn right and downhill opposite the church. Only 100m ahead, turn left into a signed public footpath beside the River Lim. Cross the lane ahead and continue into Mill Lane. Continue ahead at the next path junction. The path follows the Lim past a cottage with a waterwheel and crosses a footbridge. Again continue ahead, now with the river on your right. Follow the signs into Lyme Regis. Turn left as signed for Dinosaurland Fossil Museum and Lyme Regis Museum. Some 50m beyond Dinosaurland in Coombe Street is the Town Mill. Continue down Coombe Street to visit Lyme Fossil Shop and Lyme Regis Museum.

> **Town Mill**: The Town Mill site includes a working watermill, with guided tours of its three floors showing how the restored Victorian milling machinery and the modern hydro electric plant works. On the same site (at the time of writing) are shops, a café, dining room, brewery, pottery, art galleries and craft workshops. www.townmill.org.uk 01297 443579

6. Turn right and follow the Coastpath into Marine Parade to the Cobb. Take time to explore the Cobb, with its RNLI station and aquarium. Follow the lane uphill from the Cobb to the car park.

Right: The Cobb

> **Fossil Museum:** Housed in a Grade 1 listed former Georgian church, the museum has over 8,000 specimens, many of them local. They include ammonites and the skeletons of ichthyosaurs, dinosaurs and plesiosaurs. A time gallery explains the major geological periods and there is also a natural history room with a range of specimens. www.dinosaurland.co.uk 01297 443541 **Lyme Regis Museum** also has an excellent marine fossil collection. Its exhibits range from fossil hunter extraordinaire Mary Anning to novelists Jane Austen and John Fowles, who used Lyme as a major setting in their writings. Maritime history and the Monmouth Rebellion also feature largely. www.lymeregismuseum.co.uk 01297 443370.

2. Charmouth Distance: 8.75km/5 ½ miles, Time: 3 hours, Exertion: Demanding

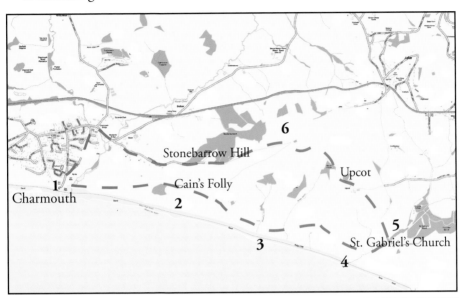

Information
Start/parking: Charmouth Beach car park SY365931, DT6 6LL
Terrain: Footpaths, bridleways, quiet lanes. Some steep ascents/descents.
Stiles: 9
Refreshments: Pubs, cafes, restaurants in Charmouth; National Trust's
Stonebarrow shop/information centre (seasonal).
Public Toilets: Charmouth
Maps: Ordnance Survey Explorer 116 or Landranger 193

Starting from Charmouth beach, this fairly demanding but very rewarding route includes splendid cliff top walking and great views east and west along the Jurassic Coast. The equally enjoyable and hilly inland return leads to the vanished medieval hamlet of Stanton St Gabriel, marked by a ruined chapel and a handsome 18th century house standing on the probable site of the medieval manor.

Pause to enjoy the superb vista from Cain's Folly (148m/489ft). Just to the east is Golden Cap, a massive cliff of Blue Lias, a Jurassic lime-stone and shale formation, capped with a golden crown of Cretaceous Greensand. At 191m/630ft, this is the highest and most impressive peak on England's South Coast. Turn west to view the great sweep of Lyme Bay – then take a vertiginous peek down the undercliff to the sea.

The view over Charmouth from the Coast Path.

Landslips made the undercliffs here and at many other points along the East Devon and West Dorset Coast. They're still making them, necessitating frequent re-alignments of the Coast Path. Every year, more pieces of the Jurassic Coast collapse – take care you don't go with them by getting too close to the crumbling cliff edge! These frequent landslips show geology as a dynamic process and yield remarkable fossils.

This extraordinarily beautiful coastline holds a unique place in science. Special credit goes to local fossil hunter Mary Anning (1799-1847). Mary discovered fossils including giant ammonites and the first two plesiosaur skeletons and gained the respect of leading Victorian geologists, despite her humble background and modest education. She thus contributed to fundamental changes in scientific thinking, especially about the Earth's antiquity, origins and development.

If you fancy a little fossil hunting yourself, start at the Charmouth Heritage Coast Centre and try the foreshore on Charmouth beach, especially the area about 200m from the river mouth. Please note that while loose fossils may be collected from the beach, removing them from the cliffs is now forbidden and can be dangerous too - Mary Anning only narrowly survived a landslip that killed her dog on one memorable collecting expedition.

If you would like a full day walk of 14.8km/9 ¼ miles, you can join this walk with Seatown West (page 10) at Point 4, which is also Point 4 on the Seatown West route. This will bring you via Seatown round to Point 5, the vanished village of Stanton St Gabriel. Simply continue the directions below back to Charmouth from there.

1 At the time of writing, the Coast Path between Charmouth and Cain's Folly (Point 2) is temporarily closed because of a landslip. When this is resolved, simply cross the river Char by the footbridge and follow the Coast Path uphill for 1.6km (1 mile) to Cain's Folly. Meantime, follow the signed diversion from the top end of the car park. Turn right along a lane. Continue along a gravel path and into Bridge Road, past the fire station to the main village road. Turn right. Cross the bridge. Fork right up Stonebarrow Lane for 1.25km to the car park at the top. Turn sharp right to a signpost, then right again. Follow the grassy path to the summit of Cain's Folly, where the extensive undercliffs testify to many earlier landslips.

2. Turn left (east) onto the Coast Path, signed "Golden Cap". Follow directional arrows around a small landslip. Follow steps downhill to a footbridge. Continue uphill.

3. You may short cut left here "Stonebarrow Hill". Otherwise, continue ahead for "Golden Cap". Descend to a footbridge. Continue uphill and then down to a stile signed "St Gabriel's Mouth".

4. Turn left for "St Gabriel's". Walk ahead to the end of the field. Cross a pair of stiles. Continue ahead past a cottage and up a stony track to a large brick and thatch building – St Gabriel's House. The ruins of St Gabriel's Chapel are ahead of you, just out of view.

5. Turn left signed "Morcombelake Stonebarrow". Do not take the turning right "Langdon Hill Morcombelake". Continue along the concrete track signed "Chardown Hill Stonebarrow". Turn left 300m ahead over a stile. Follow the left edge of the field. Exit via a pair of stiles just right of a large barn. Turn left for 100m along the track. Turn right, signed "Stonebarrow Hill Charmouth". Follow the lane uphill between houses and on to a gate. Continue ahead on the bridleway, which soon curves left, making a gentle ascent to Chardown Hill.

6. Turn left "Stonebarrow Charmouth" and follow the stony track past the National Trust's information point and shop. Follow Stonebarrow Lane steeply downhill. Meeting the road, continue ahead. Turn left down Bridge Road past the fire station. Continue down a path signed "Seafront" to the start.

3. Seatown West Distance: 6.2km/4 miles, Time: 2 ½ hours, Exertion: Demanding

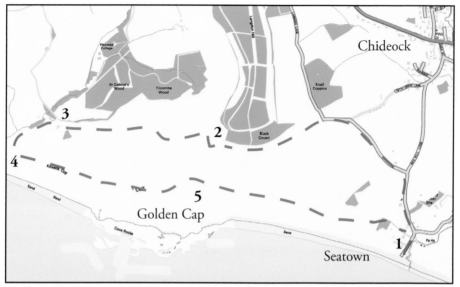

Information:
Start/parking: Seatown Beach car park SY420918, DT6 6JU
Terrain: Footpaths, bridleways, quiet lanes. One long steep ascent/descent.
Stiles: 4   **Refreshments:** Anchor Inn, Seatown, 01297 489215.
Public Toilets: Seatown   **Maps:** Ordnance Survey Explorer 116 or Landranger 193

Rising whale backed from the sea, Golden Cap looks massive from Seatown beach, the starting point for this memorable coastal route. No one walking the Jurassic Coast should miss the chance to explore Golden Cap and enjoy the superb views from the summit, both east along Chesil Bank to Portland Bill and west over Lyme Bay. At 191m/630ft Golden Cap's the highest cliff on England's South Coast – which may well have been the reason why our Bronze Age ancestors buried their dead here and honoured them with mounds. Admittedly it's not Everest, but a commendable hike up from sea level and a fair pretext for a post promenade pint at the Anchor Inn, which has an interesting medley of local photographs.

The first half of the walk includes fine views inland and the vanished medieval hamlet of Stanton St Gabriel. Eclipsed when the old coast road was superseded by the new inland turnpike road via Morcombelake (now the A35), this settlement (first recorded in Domesday

1086) is today marked by a ruined chapel and a handsome 18th century house standing on the probable site of the medieval manor.

To make a 14.8km/9 ¼ mile all day walk you can join this walk with the Charmouth and Stonebarrow Hill route (page 7) at Point 3, the vanished village of Stanton St Gabriel, which is also Point 5 on the Charmouth and Stonebarrow route. Follow that route back to Charmouth and then the directions from Charmouth to Point 4. Simply continue the directions below from there back to Seatown.

1. With your back to the sea and the Anchor Inn on your left follow the lane ahead. Ignore the footpath/bridleway on your right. Do not take the first path left (signed "Coast Path Diversion" at time of writing). Continue for 250m. Turn left into a tarred track signed "Sea Hill House". This continues uphill as a stony track (Pettycrate Lane). When the track divides, keep left and uphill.

2. Continue ahead at a junction of paths, signed "Coast Path Golden Cap", but fork almost immediately right as the bridleway divides at a gate. Reaching a second gate, continue ahead "Bridleway St Gabriel's" with the hedge on your left. Bear right (sign obscured by a thorn). Turn left at the

bottom of the field. Continue ahead past the chapel ruins to a large brick and thatch building – St Gabriel's House.

3. Continue ahead through a gate signed "To the Coast Path". This leads down a stony track past a cottage. It continues over a pair of stiles and along the left edge of the field ahead to meet a stile on the left.

4. Cross this stile signed "St Gabriel's Mouth". Continue down to the footbridge and then start the long ascent of Golden Cap.

5. Follow the Coast Path downhill from Golden Cap to a lane. Divert right to the beach and the Anchor Inn.

Left: View east from Golden Cap.

4. Seatown East Distance: 8.3km/5 ¼ miles, Time: 2 ¾ hours, Exertion: Moderate

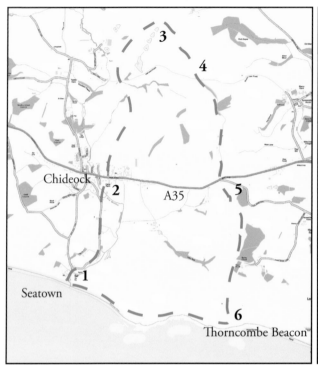

Information
Start/parking: Seatown Beach car park SY420918, DT6 6JU
Terrain: Footpaths, bridleways, quiet lanes. Three short ascents, one long descent.
Stiles: 7
Refreshments: Anchor Inn, Seatown, 01297 489215, George Inn Chideock, 01297 489419.
Public Toilets: Seatown
Maps: Ordnance Survey Explorer 116 or Landranger 193

This route offers a pleasing mix of inland and coastal walking with splendid views of both the Jurassic Coast and the West Dorset hills. Careful attention to the directions and map are needed between points 2 and 6, as waymarking is sparse in places and the paths not always obvious.

1. From Seatown beach car park take the Chideock lane. Turn right at the shop and holiday park entrance. Signed "Public Bridleway and Footpath", this is Mill Lane. Follow it past the stone built Mill House and Mill Cottage. Reaching a path junction, continue ahead "Chideock". When Mill Lane curves left, leave it and walk ahead "Public Bridleway" between hedges.

2. Cross the A35 with care. Turn right and almost immediately left into Ruins Lane and follow it to the end. Continue through a kissing gate across Ruins Field, where a crucifix marks the site of Chideock Castle (with its plaque). Cross the stile at the end of Ruins Field and continue with the hedge on your right. The field edge turns right then left to follow a line of trees to another stile. Continue with the hedge on your right and then cut

diagonally left to meet a stile at the top left corner of the field. Obscured by the hedge, it is just to the right of a corrugated iron barn. Cross this stile into what is marked on the Explorer map as Hell Lane, possibly because it can become a stream after rain! Turn left and almost immediately cross the stile high up on your right. Continue ahead with the fence on your right for 100m. Cross the stile on the right and continue with the hedge on your left as it winds to the far side of the field. Cross a farm track and head diagonally half right and uphill towards a metal gate with a blue arrow. Continue ahead and uphill as signed with a series of three ponds downhill and on your right. Exit the field by a hunting gate into a track.

3. Cross the track. Go through a second hunting gate. Turn right. Do not take the Public Bridleway on your left, but continue ahead in a south-easterly course along an enclosed track indicated by a green arrow.

4. Continue ahead into an enclosed track when you reach a junction of tracks at Quarry Cross. Almost immediately, this track divides. Keep right on the upper track. A good view of Colmer's Hill appears on the left. Named after a Rector of Symondsbury, it is a local landmark. The trees on its crown were planted there during the First World War. Continue down the hollow lane, which attains a considerable depth before joining the tarred lane at Rock Hopper. Follow this lane to the A35.

5. Cross the A35 carefully. Do not take the lane left, but follow the track ahead and uphill just left of a house. Ignore the footpath for Seatown. When the track divides, bear left and up the flank of Eype Down by a

Chideock from the footpath.

track. Turn right when you reach the summit, following a broad turf track. Enjoy the panoramic views north to Colmer's Hill (photo below), east to Bridport, south towards the sea and west along the Jurassic Coast. Continue ahead to a signed bridleway division. Turn left and continue for 200m. The track divides three ways. Turn right and sharply uphill. Turn right at the top of the slope and follow the footpath ahead into trees. Ignore side turnings. Continue to a stile with a National Trust sign "Down House Farm". Cross the stile and continue ahead with the hedge on your left to a second stile. Cross and walk ahead to Thorncombe Beacon. One of a

chain of fire beacons erected in 1588 to warn when the Spanish Armada was sighted, this beacon was restored for the 400th anniversary. There are four round barrows (prehistoric burial mounds) on Thorncombe Beacon. You may join the West Bay circular walk point 4 (page 15) on Thorncombe Beacon to make a full day figure of eight walk. 6. Turn right at Thorncombe Beacon and simply follow the Coast Path all the way to Seatown. East and west, the coastal views are terrific.

Landslips: Gazing down at the undercliffs from the top of Golden Cap, or studying its distinctive profile from Seatown beach begins to provide the explanation for landslips here and at Cain's Folly (page 9). The base of Golden Cap is a Jurassic limestone and shale formation, Blue Lias, whilst the cap of the cliff is a variety of chalk, a younger Cretaceous rock, somewhat confusingly called Greensand despite its golden colour. Separating the formations of Lias and Greensand is a thin layer of Gault Clay. Because the Greensand is pervious, rainwater seeps through it to the clay beneath. Clay is impervious, so the rainwater does not pass through it. The immense weight of Greensand formation above causes it to slide over the wet clay, resulting in a landslip. Similar rock formations west of Charmouth - Lias capped with Greensand and a top layer of clay with flints - have produced more landslips which, at the time of writing, have closed the Coast Path between Charmouth and Lyme Regis.

5. West Bay Distance: 8km/5 miles, Time: 2 ½ hours, Exertion: Moderate

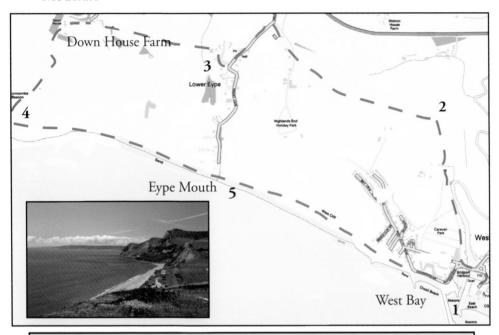

Start/parking: West Bay Harbour SY463904, DT6 4EN
Terrain: Footpaths, bridleways, quiet lanes. Steady ascent to Thorncombe Beacon; steeper descent from it.
Stiles: 4
Refreshments: Wide choice in West Bay; Down House Farm Café 01308 421232; New Inn Lower Eype 01308 423254
Public Toilets: West Bay
Maps: Ordnance Survey Explorer 116 or Landranger 193

Choose clear weather to enjoy the wonderful coastal views on this walk, which begins at West Bay's pretty harbour and climbs steadily by inland paths to Thorncombe Beacon. At 157m/518ft it's a superb viewpoint, with a vista stretching from Portland Bill in the east to Start Point in the west.

On the West Dorset coast the best views west on a sunny day are in the morning. Conversely, the best views east are later in the day. Thorncombe Beacon is on both this route and Seatown East (page 12), so it's possible to visit it twice at different times of day. Alternatively, if you're feeling energetic, the two walks can be combined to make a 16.3km/10 ¼ mile figure of eight route joined in the middle by Thorncombe Beacon – which you'll then see early and late on the same day.

1. With your back to the Bridport Arms, follow the inland side of the harbour wall. Although a harbour has existed here for centuries, the present wall dates from the 1740s. It doesn't follow a natural feature – the harbour was created by cutting a channel through the beach and excavating a basin behind. Turn right at the Salt House, where salt was stored for the local and Newfoundland fishing trades. Walk as signed through the caravan park on the Monarch's Way. Keep a straight line along the roadway. Continue ahead along a path and follow it out of the caravan park via a clump of trees and along the edge of field to a kissing gate.

2. Turn left and walk gently uphill with the hedge on your left and the steel tower in front of you. Cross a stile at the top end of the field. Continue ahead through three more fields with the hedge on your left. Cross a stile and walk along a track past the steel tower. Cross the lane ahead. Continue for 100m on "Public Bridleway". Branch left through the churchyard footpath to a lane. For the New Inn, follow the lane. Otherwise, turn left and left again over a stile and follow "Footpath to Lower Eype". Turn right and follow the lane for 75m. It dog-legs right. Turn left "Lower Eype" and follow the lane past cottages to the end and turn left along the concrete track.

West Bay Harbour

3. The bridleway divides. Branch left as signed through a concreted yard into an enclosed track. Continue through a gate and uphill towards houses. Turn left along the lane past Down House Farm Café. Continue ahead on the signed bridleway. Branch left through a metal gate just before Little Down House. Walk through one field. Cross a stile and continue ahead along the left field edge. Turn right "Eype Down Seatown" and head up to Thorncombe Beacon.

4. Thorncombe Beacon is visible for many miles, hence it was one of a chain of hilltop beacons established between the West Country and London to warn of the Spanish Armada in 1588. The brazier was restored in 1988. Less obvious are the round barrows (prehistoric burial mounds) nearby. You may join the Seatown East circular walk point 6 (page 12) here to make a full day figure of eight walk. Turn left (east) and follow the Coast Path steeply downhill from Thorncombe Beacon.

5. Follow the Coast Path east from Eype Mouth to West Bay.

6. West Bexington Distance: 6.7km/4 ¼ miles,   Time: 2 ¼ hours.
Exertion: Moderate

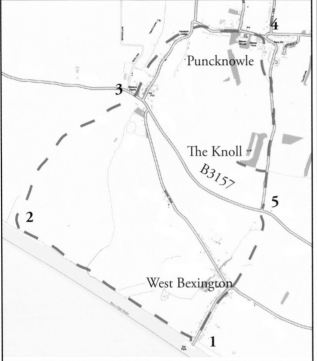

Puncknowle

The Knoll

B3157

West Bexington

Information
Start/parking: West Bexington Beach SY531865 DT2 9DG
Terrain: Footpaths, coastpath and quiet lanes. Two ascents, one descent.
Stiles: 1
Refreshments: Crown Inn, Puncknowle; Manor Hotel and beach café/shop, West Bexington.
Public toilets: At start.
Maps: Explorer OL15 or Landranger 194

Starting from West Bexington beach, this walk includes sweeping views over Lyme Bay, a Nature Reserve and two charming stone and thatch villages. Both Swyre and Puncknowle have a medieval church and Puncknowle the historic Crown Inn too. This route may be quite easily completed in a morning or an afternoon.

1. Follow the Coast Path westwards from West Bexington beach car park. This leads between the high shingle bank and the Nature Reserve with fine views along the coast to Golden Cap and beyond. Mostly reed bed and wet meadow, the reserve is a good place to spot reed and sedge warblers in summer, bearded tit, snipe and water rail in winter. Wild geraniums, sea kale and yellow horned poppy thrive on the shingle bank. Ignore the first footpath right and the second signed "Swyre". Follow the Coast Path for 300m more.
2. Turn right at the gate and follow the Public Footpath uphill with the hedge on your right to the top of the field. Bear right along the track,

which continues uphill before levelling out. Turn right along the B3157 for 100m.
3. Cross carefully and follow the lane left "Puncknowle". Divert right to see 15th century Swyre church, where the Millennium map in the porch provides a wealth of information about the parish. Particularly interesting are the field maps of 1750 and 2000. The earlier map shows many smaller fields and the remnants of medieval strip fields. Leave the church and continue on the Puncknowle lane. Reaching a junction, keep sharp right "Puncknowle". The village has a pleasing medley of stone and thatched buildings (photo below), including the Crown Inn, with its period photographs, exposed beams and log fire. Opposite is the church, which has several interesting features. Among the oldest are the 12th century font and chancel arch,

whilst the wall paintings are believed to be 14th century. The list of incumbents dates to 1321; there is a brass of 1597 and a Charles II Royal Coat of Arms, 1673.
4. Continue along the main village street. Turn right opposite Looke Lane into a public footpath, which leads uphill past a farm to a lane. Bear right and uphill. You may divert 200m right up a footpath to the top of the knoll which gave Puncknowle the second element of its name. After enjoying the view, retrace your footsteps to the lane and follow it downhill to the B3157.

In common with many English places, Swyre and Puncknowle take their names from topographical features. Whilst Swyre is derived from the Old English word "swyra", meaning a neck of land or a col, Puncknowle takes the second element of its name from the 179m/591ft high knoll (hill) south of the village. The first element is either the Old English "plume" meaning a plum-tree, or an Anglo-Saxon personal name, Puma.

5. Cross the road carefully and follow the footpath "West Bexington" downhill. Ignore the turning left "Hardy Monument" and continue downhill to a lane. Follow the lane downhill for 500m past houses to the car park.

West Bexington

7. Hardy Monument Distance: 8.3km/5 ¼ miles, Time: 2 ½ hours, Exertion: Moderate

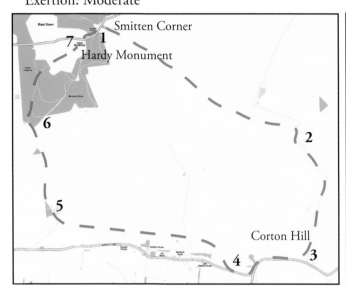

Smitten Corner

Hardy Monument

Corton Hill

Information
Start: Smitten Corner parking 250m east of Hardy Monument SY616877, DT2 9HY
Terrain: Footpaths and quiet lanes. Two ascents (one steep) and two descents.
Stiles :5
Refreshments: None en route, but pub in Portesham; choice pubs, cafés and restaurants in Abbotsbury.
Public toilets: None.
Maps: Explorer OL15 or Landranger 194

As well as magnificent views over Dorset's patchwork fields to Portland and the coast, this stimulating walk has a pleasing variety of heath, down and woodland. It also offers a good deal of historic and natural interest. The 22m (72ft) tall Hardy Monument dominates the skyline for much of the route, but the many prehistoric round barrows and shake holes on Bronkham Hill are equally impressive.

1. The parking area at the Hardy Monument is locked late afternoon, so unless you start early it is advisable to park at Smitten Corner, 250m east and down the road. (Remember to lock your car!) Take the bridlepath/Coastpath signed "Bincombe" opposite Smitten Corner parking area. Keep to the broad track and ignore side turnings. When the track divides, keep left "Bincombe". Continue past round barrows and shake holes. Ignore the bridlepath to "Martinstown" and avoid the footpaths to "Hell Bottom" and "Coryates" – both were badly overgrown at the time of writing. Continue ahead, signed "Bridlepath Corton Hill".
2. Turn right "Bridlepath Corton Hill". Look left along the ridge to see an impressive line of round barrows.
3. Reaching a lane, turn right. Continue for 600m. Follow the bend right,

signed "Portesham". Continue for 150m.

4. Turn right over a stile "Public Footpath". Walk diagonally left to the top of the steep, low ridge – a prime example of soil creep. Characteristic of Dorset's chalk downs, the terracettes formed by soil creep are mainly the result of gravity, aided by heavy rain and emphasized by generations of sheep. Eggardon Hill (page 27) and Maiden Castle (page 38) also show impressive terracettes. Continue ahead along the top of the ridge with the wall and then a fence on your right. Enjoy splendid views over the patchwork fields to the coast.

5. Turn right at a bridlepath junction and follow the track past Portesham Farm. The track rises; then descends past Black Down Barn to Benecke Wood.

6. Do not take the bridleway to Smitten Corner. Continue for 100m and turn right "Inland Route Hardy Monument". Follow the broad path uphill through trees. At a path junction, keep ahead "Hardy Monument". Erected in 1839, the Hardy Monument commemorates Rear Admiral Sir Thomas Masterman Hardy, Captain of Nelson's flagship HMS Victory at the Battle of Trafalgar in 1805. Born in 1769 at Long Bredy near Portesham, Hardy had a very distinguished career, rising to First Naval Lord at the Admiralty and Vice-Admiral of the Blue.

7. After visiting the monument and enjoying the panoramic views, follow the lane downhill to the parking area. Ahead are two impressive round barrows.

Below: The view from the Hardy Monument.

Bronze Age Barrows: Dorset's downland is a very rich prehistoric landscape and the path we follow along Bronkham Hill to Corton Down has a remarkable concentration of Bronze Age "round barrows", raised tombs built along ridge lines and on hilltops to increase their visibility. Even more were created than are now easily seen, some only surviving as crop marks. This veritable prehistoric cemetery is today covered in grass and sometimes obscured by scrub and trees, but the barrows would have stood out as gleaming white chalk when first dug between circa 2600BC and 1600BC. Round barrows succeeded the earlier long and bank barrows which were communal tombs. With their emphasis on individual burials and grave goods, they may have marked major changes in society and beliefs. Certainly, round barrows are one of the most distinctive legacies of the Bronze Age.

Bronze Age barrows on Bronkham Hill.

Shake Holes: Bronkham Hill also has many "shake holes". These are natural basins created chiefly by rainwater which, being slightly acidic, slowly dissolves the chalk below. Sinkholes of various shapes and sizes can be seen in other calcareous (chalk and limestone) formations such as the Mendips and the Yorkshire Dales.

8. Beaminster and Stoke Abbott Distance: 10km/6 ¼ miles, Time: 3 ¼ hours, Exertion: Demanding

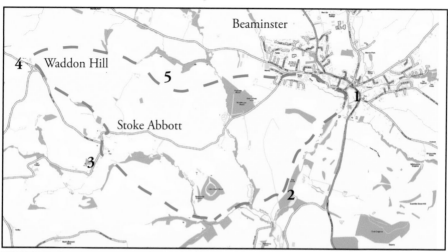

Information
Start/parking: Beaminster Square ST480013, DT8 3AU
Terrain: Footpaths, bridleways, quiet lanes. Some steep ascents/descents.
Stiles: 13
Refreshments: New Inn, Stoke Abbott; choice pubs, cafés, restaurants in Beaminster.
Public Toilets: Beaminster
Maps: Ordnance Survey Explorer 116 or Landranger 193

This exploration of rolling green hills and steep valleys offers panoramic views and a lot of historic interest - and yet you're likely to have much of the route to yourself in this little known corner of West Dorset. As a result, the paths may be overgrown in parts and attention is needed to the directions, especially between points 2 and 3 and the paths entering Beaminster at point 5. Beaminster is an intriguing town. It has a splendid church and a pleasing medley of buildings in local stone from several eras in its triangular square and neighbouring streets. En route we visit the delightful village of Stoke Abbott and pass beneath the ramparts of Waddon Hill Roman fort.

1. Start from Beaminster Square with its 1906 memorial standing on the site of the market cross. Head down Church Street, one of the most attractive in the town. Divert to see St Mary's, a 15th century church with many interesting features. These include the dignified west tower; the original

Norman font and the Strode monuments. Return to Church Street. Turn left down St Mary Well Street. Bear left along the streamside path. Turn right along the cobbled pavement for 100m. Turn second right to join a footpath. Follow the footpath over a bridge and downstream past a house and on to the end of a field. Continue into an enclosed track.

2. Turn right at a kissing gate signed for the Jubilee Trail. Cross a track. Continue ahead through a field to a gate at the lower left corner. Follow the footpath downhill over a footbridge. Turn right through a field and continue through gates. Continue along the lower edge of fields into a wood. Cross a stile and follow the path uphill to a metal gate. Continue along an enclosed path. Keep left at the first path fork. Bear right at the second fork. Almost immediately, the path forks again. This time, fork left and downhill. Follow the path (a holloway) downhill and then the track up to Stoke Abbott church. Continue to a lane.

3. Turn right. Follow the lane downhill and round the sharp right corner to the New Inn. Turn left opposite the inn into a public footpath. Follow this enclosed path uphill. Keep right when you pass a pond. Continue steeply uphill across a field to the stile at the top left corner. The ramparts of Waddon Hill Fort are clearly visible on your right. Cross the stile. Turn right up the lane to Stoke Knapp Farm.

4. Walk just beyond the farmhouse and turn right onto a signed bridleway. Bear right 50m ahead for "Chart Knole". Follow the track uphill and ahead through fields as signed to Chart Knole.

5. Take the path signed "Beaminster". Follow it uphill to the impressive beech clump on Gerrard's Hill. At 174m above sea level, its triangulation point offers a splendid panorama. Follow the path downhill towards Beaminster. Cross two stiles. Continue more steeply downhill over stiles, then uphill through trees. Follow the path diagonally across a field. Bear left along the field edge past a house and barns. Turn right and right again signed "Bridleway Footpath".

Stoke Abbott: One of Dorset's prettiest stone built villages, Stoke Abbott has a beautiful medieval church and a collection of stone built houses. Among them is the thatched 18th century New Inn. Ideally placed for a half way pint, this former farmhouse has a beer garden and a large fireplace for winter days.

Follow the field edge. Turn left along a drive "Bridleway Footpath". Turn left down a lane. Turn right into a footpath. Follow it to the church. Turn left to the square.

Gerrard's Hill

Beaminster Museum: To visit this excellent small museum turn right out of the Square and left into Whitcombe Road. Housed in a former Congregational Chapel built in 1749, the museum has a range of exhibits on local crafts and trades; archaeology; geology; domestic life and education. Check www.beaminstermuseum.org 01308 863263 for opening times and details of temporary exhibitions.

Beaminster

9. Powerstock Distance: 10.3km/6 ½ miles, Time: 3 ¼ hours, Exertion: Moderate

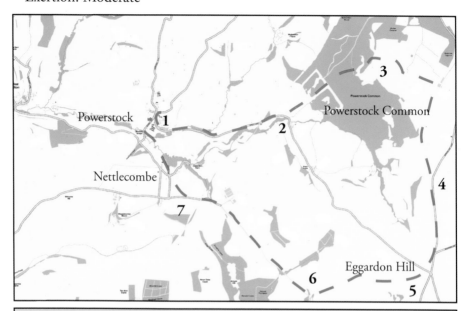

Information

Start/parking: Roadside parking with care by Powerstock church SY517962, DT6 3TF

Terrain: Footpath, bridlepaths and quiet lanes. Some ups and downs but no long or arduous slopes.

Stiles: 4

Refreshments: Three Horseshoes, Powerstock and Marquis of Lorne, Nettlecombe.

Public toilets: None **Maps:** Explorer 117 or Landranger 194

Eggardon Hill's Iron Age fort is the highlight of this exploration of a quiet and timeless corner of West Dorset. A superb viewpoint at 252m (831ft), it offers panoramic views in all directions, including a vista across Lyme Bay and on into Devon as far as Start Point. The fort covers some 8ha (20acres) and is defended by three massive ramparts with two ditches and two entrances. Inside are two Bronze Age burial mounds. Prehistoric round house foundations and storage pits have been discovered too. Later, during the Anglo-Saxon period, Eggardon Hill was used as the meeting place for the Hundred Moot, the local council or court.

Covering 115ha (284 acres), Powerstock Common Nature Reserve is the relic of a vast medieval forest where Saxon and later Norman kings hunted. Today, it is cared for by the Dorset Wildlife Trust and a haven for wildflowers, butterflies, woodland birds and elusive deer, whose slots (hoof prints) are often seen on the muddy tracks, as are badger paw marks.

We begin and end at Powerstock (pictured below), a charming village set among knolls and trees. Its beautiful church is noted for its richly ornamented Norman chancel arch, the finest in Dorset. It has many other features too, including its 15th century south doorway with carved images of the Virgin and Child.

Powerstock

1. Take the lane below Powerstock church, signed "Whetley Eggardon Hill". As King's Lane, this leads out of the village near the motte and bailey earthworks of a Norman castle and over Whetley Bridge, spanning the Bridport Railway which operated between 1857 and 1975. Follow the lane for a further 250m.
2. As the lane curves right, take "Bridleway Stones Common". This leads across a courtyard, through a gate and across a field to enter Powerstock Common. The path follows the edge of marshy ground, before entering mixed woodland, mainly oak and hazel coppice. Follow the path sign uphill to emerge into more open ground with fine views westwards.
3. Turn right at the bridleway post and hunting gate. Head across the field to a gate and turn right to the field corner. Turn left up a broad farm track and into the farmyard. Turn right as signed past Barrowland farmhouse along a track. When the track bends sharp left, cut diagonally uphill across the field ahead to a handgate in the top left corner. Turn right and follow the right field edge to the top right corner, where there is a deer spotter's

ladder. Turn left and continue along the field edge to a gateway. Go through, turn left and follow the field edge to a lane.

4. Turn right down the lane for 800m. Cross a stile on your right opposite a lane junction. Cut diagonally left across the field to a stile. Cross the lane and cut diagonally right across the next field to a metal gate. Cross a stile onto the ramparts of Eggardon Hill, where a plaque gives a brief guide to the fort's history and natural history. The steep hillside opposite is a startling example of terracetting (see Hardy Monument walk page 19).

5. Walk to the top of the ramparts to gain an impression of their massiveness and to enjoy the views. Retrace your steps to the stile. Keeping the fence on your left and the lower edge of the ramparts on your right, follow the broad track gently downhill to a small gate. Continue downhill on the bridlepath, following the right field edge.

6. Reaching North Eggardon Farm, turn right and follow the tarred track to a junction. Bear left. Follow the lane past brick piers that once carried a bridge for the Bridport Railway. Continue uphill and cross a stile on the right.

7. Follow the public footpath diagonally right across a field. Exit by a wooden gate between houses. Turn left up the lane to a junction. Turn right. Look out for an old wall plaque on one of the cottages on your right, inscribed "Dorset Rural Insurance Society. Distinct Advantages to Agricultural Workers. Local Agent." Continue to the Marquis of Lorne, a handsome stone built inn with a good collection of period photographs. Turn right beside the inn and follow the right field edge downhill to a gate and on through trees to a footbridge. Cross and continue half way across the field. Turn right through a small gate, cross a footbridge and follow the path uphill to a lane. Turn left and return to the start – or stop for refreshment at the Three Horseshoes.

Eggardon Hill

10. Abbotsbury Distance: 9.3km/5 ¾ miles, Time: 3 hours, Exertion: Moderate

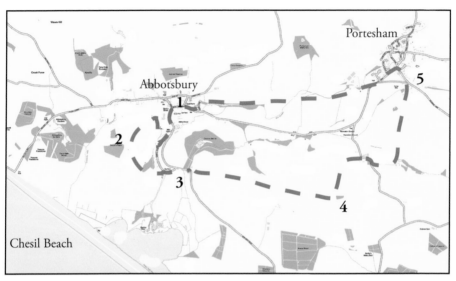

Information
Start/parking: Signed car park on eastern edge of Abbotsbury by B3157 SY 579853, DT3 4JL
Terrain: Mainly footpaths with short sections of pavements and quiet lanes. Some short but fairly steep slopes.
Stiles: 9
Refreshments: Pubs, cafés and restaurants in Abbotsbury; Royal Oak, Portesham.
Public toilets: Abbotsbury   **Maps:** Explorer OL15 or Landranger 194

An exceptionally attractive stone built village, Abbotsbury is best explored and appreciated on foot. This walk includes Abbotsbury's key historic sites and great views from Chapel Hill and the ridge path, before visiting Portesham and making a pleasant return along the old railway.

Abbotsbury grew around the 11th century Abbey. Although this was largely destroyed during Henry VIII's Dissolution of the Monasteries (1536-40), there are quite substantial ruins along Church Street, where some of the beautiful masonry has been re-used in other buildings. The Abbey's Tithe Barn is its most impressive survival. One of the largest in England at 272ft (82.5m) long, it dates from around 1400. Along with its ancient pond, it is now a children's farm.

St Catherine's Chapel (photo below) was probably built as a pilgrim chapel at about the same time as the Tithe Barn. Perched boldly on its hill, it survived Henry VIII's Dissolution of the Monasteries because it was a valuable seamark. Buttresses and stone roof give an impression of mass and strength reinforced by the vaulted interior.

1. Turn left out of the car park into Rodden Row, with its medley of stone and thatch or slate roofed 18th and 19th century listed cottages. Turn left again into Church Street. St Nicholas's has many interesting features including a stone effigy of an abbot in the porch; a 1638 chancel ceiling with beautiful plasterwork; gilded reredos and a fine brass chandelier. Continue down Church Street past Abbey House, which stands on the site of the old monastic infirmary and incorporates stone from the abbey. Continue to the Tithe Barn. Branch right along the lane (Grove Lane) signed "Swannery Pedestrians" and continue past houses. Turn right over a stone stile. Follow the path right. Keep right "Abbotsbury St Catherine's Chapel". Reaching a gate, turn sharp left "St Catherine's Chapel". Looking back on the uphill path there are splendid views of Abbotsbury, especially on a summer's evening when long shadows pick out the details and define the strip lynchets (medieval cultivation terraces) on the slope.
2. Take the path on the chapel's south-east side "Coast Path and Swannery". Head over the turf, aiming for the southern edge of Chapel Coppice. Pick up a steep path downhill at the edge of the coppice. Follow this down to a wall gate. Cross a stile ahead and continue around the side of a house to the Swannery entrance. Abbotsbury Swannery (admission charge) has up to 600 birds and is the oldest managed swan population in the world, first recorded in 1393. Either visit or continue ahead "Coast Path Weymouth" to a lane. Turn right "Coast Path" and continue for 150m.

3. Turn left over a stile "Coast Path Ferry Bridge". Cross another stile at the top of the field and continue via a series of waymarks to the top of the ridge. Continue along the ridge path, enjoying fine views of Chesil Bank, the Fleet and the

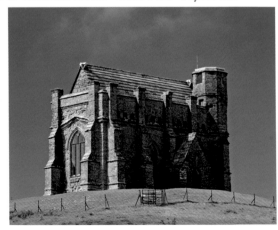

Abbotsbury

Swannery. The ridge path continues via field edges, scrub and four more stiles.

4. Reaching a path junction, leave the Coast Path by turning left through a metal gate. The enclosed path leads over the top of the ridge and downhill to a track junction. Turn right and follow the track to West Elworth, a splendid stone and thatch house. Turn right, signed "East Elworth" and follow the lane around a right hand bend. Turn left "East Elworth" along a concrete track. Fork left when this divides. Walk past a converted barn and turn left at a path division. Keep the hedge on your right. Cross the stile ahead and keep the hedge on your right. Continue past a caravan site to the B3157.

5. Turn left and cross the road. Follow the pavement as it bends sharp left at the King's Arms. At the end of the pavement, turn right "Abbotsbury". Ignore the first (concrete) track on the right. Take the second track right, a broad stony track which follows the old railway along embankments and then through wooded cuttings. This branch line linked Abbotsbury and Portesham to the busier Weymouth line between 1885 and 1952. Continue past the old engine shed to meet the B3157. Turn right and follow the pavement back to the car park. Abbotsbury's galleries, craft studios and shops are well worth exploring and there's a good choice of places to eat and drink, including the Ilchester Arms, a grand coaching inn.

11. Portland Bill Distance: 6.9km/4 ¼ miles, Time: 2 hours, Exertion: Easy

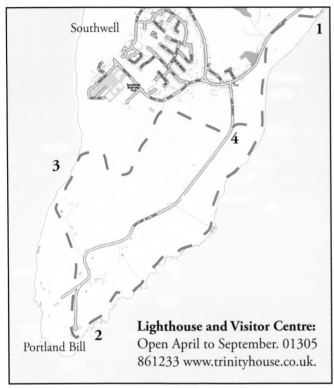

Southwell

1

4

3

Portland Bill

2

Lighthouse and Visitor Centre:
Open April to September. 01305
861233 www.trinityhouse.co.uk.

Information
Start/parking:
Cheyne Weare's car
park, on Easton/
Southwell road
SY693 705, DT5
2EG
Terrain:
Coastpath,
footpath and
pavement. Mainly
level or near level.
Stiles: 2
Refreshments:
Café at Portland
Bill.
Public toilets:
Portland Bill
Maps: Explorer
OL15 or
Landranger 194

Although short, this walk around Portland Bill is packed with interest and great coastal views. En route we visit Portland Lighthouse and its visitor centre, as well as disused quarries where cranes and stone blocks, many bearing the marks of quarrymen's tools, speak eloquently about Portland's tough industrial history.

Jutting out into the English Channel, the Isle of Portland is the major landmark of the Dorset coast but, with its rocks and dangerous currents, it has always been a hazard and the graveyard of many ships. Portland's first lighthouses were established in 1716 when two towers with enclosed lanterns and coal fires were constructed by Trinity House. The currently used 41m/ 135ft tall red and white tower dates from 1906 and is regularly open to the public. Climbing its 153 steps is rewarded with splendid coastal views.

The Visitor Centre adjoins Portland Bill Lighthouse. There are helpful staff, books, gifts and exhibits on Portland Stone, geology and fossils;

The coast path towards Portland Bill

explanatory plaques and audio visual displays. Live action from cameras focused on sea bird nests on the Hidden Ledges are a special feature.

Portland Bill is renowned not only for seabirds, but also for birds of prey, especially kestrels. Large numbers of migrating birds use the Bill as a navigation mark in spring and autumn and the old Lower Lighthouse is a bird observatory.

Scenery and wildlife draw most visitors to Portland, making tourism its leading industry, but quarrying remains important. Portland's oolitic limestone has long been prized by masons for its durability and carving qualities. It was used in Exeter Cathedral in the 14th century, but its fame spread in the 17th century after Inigo Jones used Portland Stone in the Whitehall Banqueting House and Sir Christopher Wren employed it in St Paul's Cathedral. Portland limestone was later used in Buckingham Palace and production rose to new heights with the Victorian building boom. Quarries are scattered over the island, but much stone is now mined, reducing the industry's impact on the environment greatly.

1. Enjoy the coastal views from the car park, where a plaque gives details of Portland's fascinating geology and quarrying history. Turn left out of the car park, "Coast Path Portland Bill". Follow the roadside verge, and then cross to the pavement opposite. Re-cross the road and follow the signed Coastpath through disused quarries. Look back for a superb view of Freshwater Bay with Weymouth Bay beyond. Follow the Coastpath along the low cliff top past Cave Hole, old quarry cranes and chalets (a

characteristically British seaside addition) to the lighthouse and visitor centre.

2. From the lighthouse, head across the car park to a fingerpost marked "Coastpath Chiswell". This leads over the turf to the National Coastwatch lookout, where visitors are welcome, subject (of course) to operational demands. The Coastwatch volunteers at Portland cover 1658 square km/640 square miles, including Portland Race and the Shambles Banks with their dangerous currents. It is essentially a visual watch, but backed by radar and AIS (Automatic Identification System). A vital service, the Coastwatch relies entirely on voluntary contributions. Continue along the cliff top path to a waymark just short of a high wire fence.

3. Turn right, signed "East Cliff". Keep left when the path divides. When the track curves sharp left, keep left and follow the track between dry stone walls. These walls, characteristic of Portland and Purbeck, also separate a series of small fields. Just before you reach a road, turn right over a stile. Follow the footpath path ahead and continue over the next stile, signed "East Cliff".

4. Turn right along the roadside pavement for 160m. Turn right onto "Public Footpath". Turn left "Coastpath" and retrace your steps through the disused quarry and back along the pavement and verge to the start.

The coast to the east of Portland Bill.

12. Osmington   Distance: 4.8km/3 miles,   Time: 1 ½ hours,
Exertion: Easy

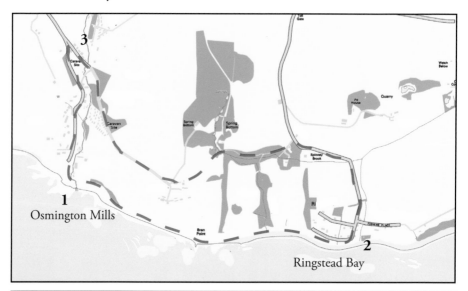

Information
Start/parking: Smugglers Inn car park, Osmington Mills SY735816, DT3 6HF
Terrain: Coastpath, footpaths and quiet lanes. A few ups and downs, but no long or tough slopes. **Stiles:** 0
Refreshments: Smugglers Inn, Osmington Mills and beach café, Ringstead.
Public toilets: Osmington Mills and Ringstead
Maps: Explorer OL15 or Landranger 194

Beginning at the aptly named Smugglers Inn, this gentle walk includes beautiful views westwards over Weymouth Bay and eastwards to the chalk headland of White Nothe. Both Osmington and Ringstead have attractive beaches for a picnic or a dip in the briny, whilst the varied Jurassic rock formations at Osmington are well worth exploring, especially at low tide.

Known as the Crown until the 1970s, the Smugglers Inn was owned by Emmanuel Charles in the late 18th and early 19th centuries. Smuggling – or "Free Trade" as its practitioners preferred to call it – was at its height whilst the attention of the armed forces and the government was distracted by war. Emmanuel Charles combined running the pub with fishing and smuggling. It was nothing unusual then for a landlord to have an additional trade and sailing a perfectly legal fishing boat provided a good cover for illegal contraband sailings across the Channel. No doubt, the Crown supplied duty free French brandy and tobacco at very reasonable prices.

The Smugglers Inn

Charles did good business with French smuggler Pierre Latour, aka French Pete, war between their respective nations notwithstanding. Latour and his boat L'Hirondelle (the Swallow) were eagerly sought by Poole Revenue. The story goes that a zealous young Preventive Officer, John Tallman, visited the Crown to pump Emmanuel Charles for information about the Frenchman. Charles plied him with brandy and painted such a picture of Latour's ferocity that Tallman grew increasingly fearful. When L'Hirondelle cast anchor in the bay, the landlord offered to hide Tallman in the inn's chimney.

French Pete strode into the bar for his usual friendly glass of grog but, having been tipped the wink by Charles, decided the evening was chilly and asked for the fire. It was duly lit and a choking, shame faced Preventive was soon forced to reveal himself. Perhaps for fear of ridicule, he may have let the matter lie.

Emmanuel Charles's relations were much involved in the Free Trade. His brother, John, died in a shipping accident, possibly a smuggling run, in 1809 and his son, Richard, was shot by the Coastguard off Purbeck in 1835. It appears that Emmanuel was a ringleader for the Charles clan and at least 27 of his extended family were convicted smugglers, punished variously with fines, imprisonment in Dorchester Gaol or (perhaps worse) service in the Royal Navy.

It is no coincidence that Osmington Mills gained two Coastguard stations, the first in 1835, and the second in 1911. Focused on fishing and, with the arrival of the charabanc trade in the early 20th century, on tourism, Osmington has thrived.

1. Take the signed Coastpath "Ringstead" out of the car park and down steps to the Smugglers Inn, which has an interesting collection of period

photographs. Bear left around the inn and up a tarred path. Continue uphill through two kissing gates, enjoying the views westwards. Stop just before you reach a brick observation post and look carefully down the cliff: low tide reveals the ribs of a wrecked ship, her form defined by seaweed and sand. When the path divides, keep ahead "Coastpath Ringstead". Descend the steps. At low tide, you may divert right and walk along the beach to Ringstead, though walking on pebbles is tiring! If you follow the beach, return to the Coastpath when you reach a concrete ramp. Otherwise, simply follow the Coastpath on to Ringstead. When the path bends left, follow it on to the beach kiosk and car park.

2. Follow the tarred track ahead. It bends left and just beyond a house, right. Only 100m beyond this, turn left "Public Footpath". Follow the stony track to a bend. Turn right through a gate. Continue ahead at a path junction, signed "Upton Osmington Mills". A pleasant wooded path, this leads over a brook and across fields. Continue between cottages, along a tarred track and past the back of a caravan park.

3. Reaching the lane, turn left and follow it downhill to the start. Divert onto the beach. The clays, sandstones and limestones here were deposited under shallow seas during the Upper Jurassic, around 155 million years ago and the sea has helped carve them into ridges, boulders and shelves. (See *The Jurassic Coast Illustrated*, Robert Westwood, 2008 for a full description).

Osmington Mills

13. Maiden Castle Distance: 7.6km/4 ¾ mile, Time: 2 ½ hours, Exertion: Easy

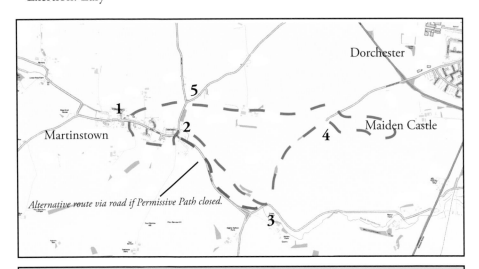

Information
Start/parking: Roadside parking with care by Martinstown church SY648890, DT2 9HY
Terrain: Footpath, bridlepaths and quiet lanes. A few ups and downs, but no long or really steep slopes.
Stiles: 3
Refreshments: Brewer's Arms, Martinstown; Steven's Farm Shop, Martinstown.
Public toilets: None   **Maps:** Explorer OL15 or Landranger 194

Starting at Martinstown with its historic church and thatched cottages, this walk includes a 2.5km (1 ½ mile) circuit of Maiden Castle's formidable outer ramparts. Britain's largest and most strongly defended Iron Age town, Maiden Castle covers 19ha (47 acres); its massive banks and ditches hewn from rock and earth.

Beginning as a small causewayed Neolithic camp about 3000 BC, Maiden Castle developed in three phases. It was reconstructed on a much larger scale around 350BC with a single bigger rampart and two gateways. Around 250BC the camp was greatly extended again to its present size of 19ha. It was greatly re-fortified between 150 and 70BC when the early single rampart was heightened and two additional circuits were built with stone revetments and cores, further strengthened by outworks. As a demonstration of the political and military power of the Durotriges, the Celtic tribe who gave Dorset its name, it must have been fearsome.

Nonetheless, Vespasian and the Legio II Augusta stormed it in AD44. A British skeleton with a Roman ballista bolt embedded in its spine rests in Dorchester Museum, testimony to the violent battle, whilst the thousands of unused British slingstones recovered from Maiden Castle indicate the Durotriges' determination to resist the best trained, disciplined and armed force of the ancient world.

The 21st century is not far away: Maiden Castle overlooks Poundbury. A phased expansion of Dorchester using innovative design, Poundbury is the brain child of the Prince of Wales and the ideas he championed in his *Vision of Britain* (1989). Work started on Poundbury in the mid 1990s and it is hoped to complete in 2025, by which time it will accommodate around 5,000 people.

1. With your back to Martinstown church gate, take the signed Public Bridleway almost opposite – just to the left of a terrace of thatched cottages. Follow the track uphill for 300m. Turn left and follow the Public Footpath with the fence on your left. Cross a lane and stile. Continue along the

field edge to a lane. Cross and turn left to follow the further of two tracks beside a thatched cottage to a junction.

2. Take the Dorchester road ahead for only 70m. Turn right to join "Permissive Bridleway" at a metal gate beside "Four Acres". (This is not marked on 2004 Explorer map.) Cross the field to a gate, and then follow the left edge of a large field ahead. Continue ahead as signed with South Winterbourne on your right, ignoring side turnings.

Common on the Dorset downs, "winterbournes" are seasonal chalk streams, usually flowing only in winter – though South Winterbourne was flooded in the exceptionally wet summer of 2012, despite its name.

3. Continue up to a lane, but do not take it. Turn left and follow "Public Bridlepath" up a steep sided valley. Turn right over a stile and follow the narrow path up to the outer ramparts. Turn right and walk along the top of the ramparts anti-clockwise for the next 2.5km (1 ½ miles) – an almost complete circuit. Reaching a stile, cross over and turn right where a plaque explains this is the Western Entrance and a drawing shows its intricate construction, designed to confuse attackers and make them more vulnerable. With your back to the plaque, cross the two low ramparts ahead and exit by a small gate.

4. Turn right down the sunken track for 100m. Turn left onto a path and keep the fence on your right. The path turns sharp right and heads downhill to a crosstracks, close to a very large round barrow. Turn left onto a broad track "Cycle Route 2". Follow the well-signed track between farm buildings. Continue to meet a road.

5. Cross the road and the lane in front of it to join a bridleway at a gate. Continue ahead along the left field edge, through a gate and along the left edge of the next field. Turn left down a tarred track. Turn right to the church.

Opposite and below: The ramparts of Maiden Castle.

14. Plush Distance: 7km/4 ½ miles, Time: 2 ¼ hours, Exertion: Moderate

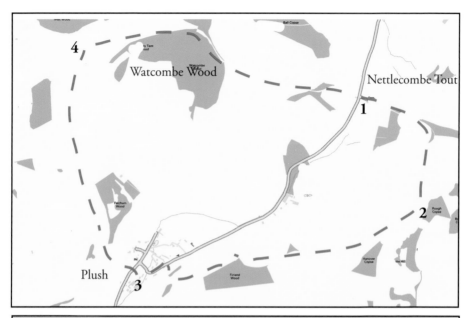

Information
Start/parking: Roadside parking with care at Folly Lane crossing ST728032, DT2 7RN 2 miles north of Plush and 2 miles south of Mappowder on Piddletrenthide/Plush/Mappowder road.
Terrain: Bridlepaths, footpaths and quiet lanes. Two moderate ascents and descents.
Stiles: 3
Refreshments: Brace of Pheasants, Plush.
Public toilets: None **Maps:** Explorer OL117 or Landranger 194

Following bridlepaths and footpaths, this route explores the beautiful chalk downland north of Dorchester. As well as wide views over the rounded hills there is a fine view of the gentler country of Blackmore Vale from the Wessex Ridgeway, which forms the northern part of the walk.

An ancient highway running from Lyme Regis across Dorset and north east to Holme on the Norfolk coast, the Wessex Ridgeway is a superb long distance path. Also of historic interest are the cross dykes on Lyscombe Hill and the prehistoric settlement and field system on West Hill and Church Hill; whilst the 16th century Brace of Pheasants provides welcome refreshments half way at the delightful hamlet of Plush.

Above: The village of Plush.

1. Park carefully on the verge at Folly. The house on the west side of the road used to be a drovers' inn called The Fox, whilst the lane crossing was part of a network of drovers' tracks. It is also part of the Wessex Ridgeway and thus rooted deep in Britain's pre-Roman history. Take the track opposite the house signed "Dorset Gap". Follow it eastwards for 400m. When the track forks, keep right to a gate and stile. Follow the sunken track ahead. This curves gently right and uphill to a cross tracks on Lyscombe Hill.

2. Continue along the ridge, signed "Dole's Ash Farm". Look carefully for the "cross dykes" marked on Ordnance Survey maps. These are traces of Bronze Age field systems. The clearest example is 50m beyond the triangulation pillar on Higher Hill. From there continue through two gates as signed to a large field. Although the bridlepath and footpath run across the field it was ploughed at the time of writing. Therefore, turn right and keep the field edge on our right, being careful to avoid trampling any crops. Reaching the corner of the field, turn left and keeping Firland Wood on your right continue to the far corner. Turn left and uphill for 80m along the field edge. Turn right over a stile and right again to follow the field edge to a wire fence. Turn left and follow the fence to another stile. Cross and follow the path steeply downhill to a lane. Turn left and follow the lane to the Brace of Pheasants.

3. Turn left and follow the lane towards Piddletrenthide for only 60m. Turn right up a broad track signed "Church Hill" and climb steadily to a metal gate. Continue along the ridge track for only 100m to a low stone marker on West Hill. On the slope to your right are clear traces of a medieval strip field system imposed on an earlier prehistoric one covering some 79ha (190acres). Fork left here, continuing gently uphill to meet the Wessex Ridgeway on Church Hill – the track as it is diverges slightly east (right) to the line marked on the Explorer map to meet a stile. Do not cross the stile, but enjoy the view north to Blackmore Vale. A helpful plaque explains how Harvey's Farm has been improved for wildlife through environmental schemes.

4. Turn right along the Ridgeway, keeping the hedge on your left. Look out for a low raised bank and adjoining ditch some 500m ahead on your right. Approximately 40m square, this enclosure is part of a prehistoric or Romano-British settlement. Just beyond is a round dew pond. Continue on the Wessex Ridgeway through a metal gate and on through woodland. Exit the woodland via a gate and continue ahead on the Ridgeway as signed, keeping the field edge on your left. Go through another gate and follow the path downhill through scrub to the start.

Although many English inns are named after birds, the Brace of Pheasants has a very unusual if not unique name and a unique sign. A pair of pheasants in a glass case stand over the door, put there by local taxidermist, bon viveur, tipster and clock maker David Green, maker of the famous Cerne Abbas clocks with their distinctive second "hands". Built of brick and flint in the 16th century, the Brace of Pheasants was originally two cottages and a forge belonging to the Hankey estate. It only became an inn in the 1930s and was originally the Hankey Arms. The inn has an interesting collection of local period photographs and beer from the barrel.

The Brace of Pheasants in Plush.

15. Cerne Abbas Distance: 10.3km/6 ½ miles, Time: 3 ¼ hours, Exertion: Moderate

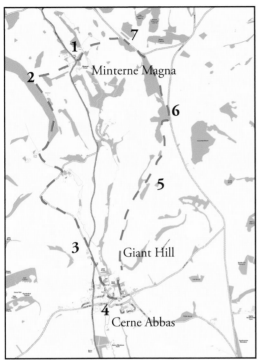

Information
Start/parking: Roadside car park opposite Minterne Magna church ST659043, DT2 7AS
Terrain: Bridlepaths, footpaths, quiet lanes and short road section. Two ascents and descents.
Stiles: 2
Refreshments: Choice of inns and cafés in Cerne Abbas.
Public toilets: Cerne Abbas
Maps: Explorer OL117 or Landranger 194

This exploration of the beautiful Cerne Valley has a great deal of historic interest. Up Cerne and Minterne Magna are attractive villages, whilst Cerne Abbas has a remarkable medley of historic buildings in brick, stone and timber. Its abbey, tithe barn and church are particularly interesting.

For all that, the most memorable and unusual sight on the walk is the Cerne Abbas Giant, an unmistakably triumphant and phallic symbol whose age and origins have been much debated. Cut into the chalk hillside, the Giant is 180ft long, 167ft wide and brandishes a club 120ft long in his right hand. Despite his size, he could not have survived without regular attention to keep back encroaching weeds.

Most probably the Giant is Romano-British in origin, though the

earliest record of his existence only dates from 1742. He is thought to be a British Hercules, a cult figure symbolizing strength and fertility. Certainly, he resembles Roman coins, statuettes and Castor ware representing Hercules. He may well date from the time of the Roman Emperor Commodus (AD180-93). After defeating the Scots in 187, Commodus declared himself Hercules incarnate and added Hercules Romanus to his titles.

However, it is impossible to be sure whether the Giant we see today is the true original or one modified (or possibly designed) by later and maybe ruder hands; especially as other British chalk cut figures, including the Wilmington Long Man in Sussex and the Uffington White Horse in Oxfordshire, show some change of form and character over the centuries. For many, the unanswered questions surrounding the Giant add to his appeal.

1. Take the bridleway beside the green behind Minterne Magna's car park. Follow the directional arrows right, then left. Continue on a broad track uphill between fields to wooded East Hill.
2. Turn left onto the bridlepath. After 500m the path divides. Fork right and downhill to a lane. Turn left and follow the lane to Up Cerne. Turn right and follow the lane for 1.4km (1 mile) to the main road.
3. Turn right and follow the verge carefully. Turn left to the Giant's Viewpoint. Follow the lane to the main village street. Turn right in front of the New Inn, a late 17th/18th century coaching inn. Follow the street past the telephone booth. Take the first footpath left signed "Barton Meadows Farm". Do not enter the private drive, but the tithe barn may be viewed from the footpath. Built in the 14th century, it was converted to a private dwelling in the 18th century.
4. Retrace your steps to the New Inn. Continue along the main street

(Long Street) to the Royal Oak. This delightful thatched building has an early 16th century core with 18th and 19th century alterations. Features include period photographs, exposed beams, flagstones and an open fire.

Turn left to visit the church. Originally built by the monks about 1300, it has medieval wall paintings, a splendid Jacobean pulpit and a 15th century stone screen.

Continue along Abbey Street. Cerne Abbey is a private house incorporating parts of the medieval monastic gatehouse, but largely rebuilt from the 18th century. Go through the gate (admission charge) to see the Abbey Guest House and the Abbot's porch with its lovely oriel windows. Plaques explain the history of the abbey. Retrace your steps to the entrance. From the entrance to Cerne Abbey, turn through a stone arch. Bear left along the footpath through the graveyard. Keep left when the path divides. Bear left and up steps signed "Giant Hill". The path continues beneath the Giant, gaining height gently and then more steeply, before levelling out.
5. Cross a stile and take the path ahead across the field, signed "Wessex Ridgeway". Reaching a crosstracks at the field corner continue ahead "Giant Walk" with the wood on your left. Turn left "Minterne Parva" at the next crosstrack. Cross the field to another crosstrack. Turn right "Barnes Lane". Keep the trees on your left to a metal gate. Continue ahead, still with the trees on your left and on through a small wood.
6. Just before you reach the road, turn left at a stile and gate signed "Minterne Magna". Go through the small wooden gate ahead. Continue along the field edge with the trees on your left to eventually meet a track. Turn left "Minterne Magna". Only 50m ahead is another crosstrack. Continue ahead "Minterne Magna".
7. Turn left at the gate signed "Minterne Magna". Follow the path as it curves gently downhill to a small gate in the lower field edge between

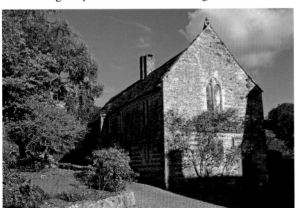

two clumps of trees. Continue downhill through a gate and on with the field edge on your right. Cross a ford and follow the lane up to the car park.

Pg 44: The Cerne Valley. Left: The Abbot's Guest House, part of the old abbey.

16. Sherborne Distance: 8km/5miles, Time: 2 ½ hours, Exertion: Easy

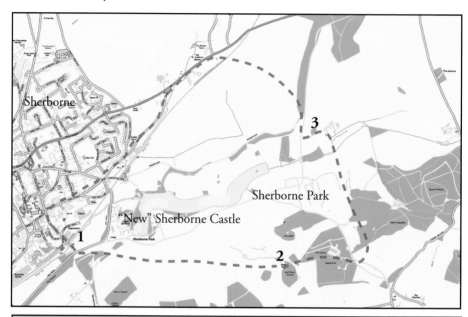

Information

Start/parking: Car park off Ludbourne Road near Sainsburys ST 642164, DT9 3NJ

Terrain: Bridleways, footpaths, some road walking but on footpaths, gentle ascents.

Stiles: 4

Refreshments: Pubs, cafés and restaurants in Sherborne.

Public toilets: In car park at start. **Maps:** Explorer 129 or Landranger 183

With its buildings of golden Jurassic limestone and dominated by the graceful abbey, Sherborne is one of Dorset's most beautiful towns. It takes its name from the Old English "scire-burne" meaning "clear stream", an apt description of the lovely River Yeo which runs through the town. In AD 705 King Ine of Wessex appointed Aldhelm as the first Bishop of Sherborne and the town's importance grew further after Roger de Caen, Chancellor to Henry I, built a castle here in the early 12th century. The walk takes in lovely countryside on the outskirts of the town and affords great views of "new" Sherborne Castle and its parkland. At the end of the walk why not wander around the town, visit the abbey and stop for refreshment in one of Sherborne's many pubs and restaurants.

1. This walk starts by the railway level crossing at the end of South Street. There is a car park nearby off Ludbourne Road opposite Sainsburys. Cross over the B3145 (New Road) and you will see a footpath directly opposite over a stile. Take this path and turn left towards Sherborne Castle. Keep following the path; it will take you across open fields with great views of the castle and its parkland. You will come to a small lodge by a wooded area.

2. Continue up the hill and bear right at the top, continuing to follow the path. You will go through an enclosed wooded area past some farm buildings. Turn left at the end on a small road and follow the path, turning right as you reach the drive of a small cottage and then left through a wooded area. The path now descends through a deer park. Keep straight on and cross the stream at the bottom.

3. You will reach the tiny hamlet of Pinford; turn left and then right across a field. Go through the big gateway at the top and follow the path through the woods. Turn left out of the woods after a short way and follow the path across the fields, under the railway to the A30. You can then follow this the short distance back into Sherborne, following the signs for the town centre. There is a footpath all the way. When you reach the A30 be sure, first, to have a look at the ancient chancel of Saint Cuthbert.

"New" Sherborne Castle

In 1594 Sir Walter Raleigh started work on a new castle in the deer park of the old one. In 1617 Sir Walter's creation was acquired by Sir John Digby, Earl of Bristol. Digby was a Royalist but retained the castle after defeat by the Parliamentarians and the Digby family (now the Wingfield-Digbys) have held it ever since.

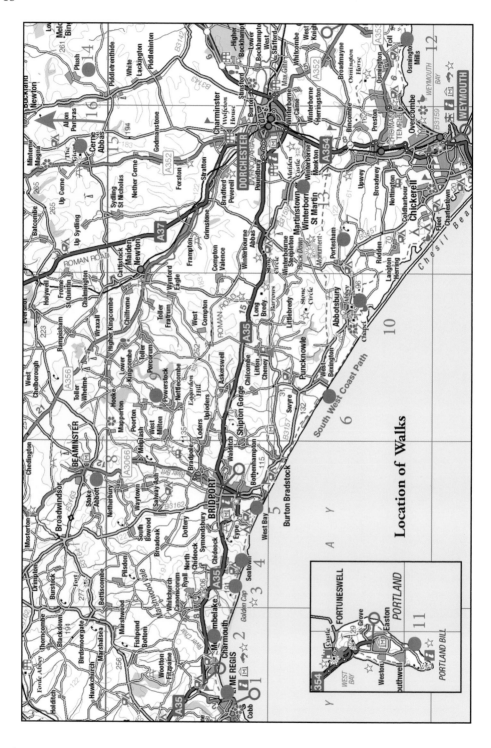

Location of Walks